For

New Beginnings

New Beginnings

✦

Jeffrey S. Martin

iUniverse, Inc.
New York   Bloomington

New Beginnings

The views expressed in this work are solely those of the author and do not necessarily reflect the views of the publisher, and the publisher hereby disclaims any responsibility for them.

iUniverse books may be ordered through booksellers or by contacting:

iUniverse
1663 Liberty Drive
Bloomington, IN 47403
www.iuniverse.com
1-800-Authors (1-800-288-4677)

Because of the dynamic nature of the Internet, any Web addresses or links contained in this book may have changed since publication and may no longer be valid.

ISBN: 978-1-4502-0361-6 (sc)
ISBN: 978-1-4502-0362-3 (ebk)

Printed in the United States of America

iUniverse rev. date: 04/19/2010

New Beginnings

Do you ever get the feeling that something is missing in life, that this can't be it? You've worked hard all your life ... for this? Isn't there supposed to be inspiration, purpose and meaning in your life?

You know those moments when goose bumps ride down your spine, making you shiver and you instinctively smile? The poems and reflections in this book are designed to give you access to such moments. These feelings indicate you are alive and in touch with inspiration, purpose, and meaning. Find that state, smile and be with it. Someone may smile back at you too. Build those shiver moments into every day, and watch. From this perspective you will see that place where life has inspiration and meaning.

Build this inspiration into each day, and share it with others. That may be the person in the bed beside you at the homeless shelter, the person who is short of change at the store, or the person on the side of the road with a flat tire. Fill the void in your life by identifying your abilities, your strengths, your connection to God, and extend these to those around you. As you extend yourself, others will instinctively be there for you too. Now that is a purpose for life!

This collection is dedicated to family members, friends, countless therapists, speakers such as Dr. Wayne Dyer and Collette Barron Reid, and many angels I have encountered along my life's path. They have been by my side and have been a great support to me as I've climbed the mountains in my life. Several of the inspirations you will read in the following pages have come to me during seminars with some of these people and while studying the inspirations they have brought. The Landmark Education Seminar Series in Toronto has also been an important part of this process for me.

Take a journey through these pages of poetry and spiritual reflections, to the place of serenity, which lies within each of us. Open yourself up to inspiration and see where the next step takes you.

A Compass for 'New Beginnings'

The Last Straw

✦

Jeff Martin is a survivor. Amid the struggles of every day, he focuses on the possibilities and uses them as his guide. His character was shaped by what he found behind his inner doors (his true character, ability, and connection with God).

Jeff has been tested throughout his life. He was born a few weeks premature and had to overcome spinal meningitis at an early age. He was a solitary child who hesitated to play with other children during recess time or to answer questions in class, for fear of being ridiculed. He lacked self-confidence and became very withdrawn in social situations.

Jeff was a tall, skinny, blond-haired, accident-prone boy. He was always the last to be chosen for sports teams or class projects. People often overlooked his ability. He was dogged by clumsiness and bad luck: he fell off a teeter-totter and needed twelve stitches; during recess time he tripped and fell onto the top of the school well sticking out of the ground, dislocating his hip. He was punched in the face and had his jaw broken during a basketball game in gym class and was hit by a car during a school bike-athon. More recently, Jeff was in a life-threatening motorcycle accident.

Jeff grew up in the quaint town of Winterbourne, just outside of Kitchener-Waterloo Ontario. If your neighbor's rooster didn't wake you up, the familiar sound of horse's hooves might. This small hamlet had lots of character and charm. Every day, horse-drawn buggies rode through the small town of just over 500 people, past the local church that had a hand-cranked bell to notify townspeople when services were about to begin. Mennonites walked along the roadside as they traveled to and from farms where their days work would begin. Growing up in this small, intimate environment, Jeff developed an appreciation for the simple things in life and for family and friends.

Jeff went to the same high school his father had attended; Rockway Mennonite Collegiate in Kitchener, Ontario. Jeff thrived in his studies but particularly loved outdoor sports. During high school Jeff developed athletic abilities and the accident-prone boy seemed to be set aside. He excelled in track and field and cross-country running. This newly developed ability was now a daily passion. Following high school he went to McMaster University in Hamilton, Ontario, where he studied Kinesiology, in the hopes of becoming a physical-education teacher. During spring break in this first year at university, Jeff was involved in a serious motorcycle accident. Coming off a motorcycle at over 100 km/hr, he hit a tree with his head and shoulder and was put into a coma for six weeks. Additionally, during two of these weeks he was on life support. This impact collapsed his lungs and fractured his C1 vertebrae. That was the last straw before Jeff began creating his own life, his way.

After the accident Jeff was rushed to Kitchener-Waterloo hospital where he remained for eleven months. In the initial stages of his intense rehabilitation, he could only remain awake for five minutes at a time before slipping back to sleep again. Literally, Jeff would be talking to someone, and he would not be capable of continuing consciousness any longer. He did the best he could when talking, but his lungs had collapsed in the accident and were still very weak. This extreme exhaustion which he experienced over his whole body as well as severe short-term memory problems, the inability to walk, and the inability to control which thoughts and ideas he acted out and which ideas he kept to himself (severe impulse control issues) are only a few of the effects he has experienced and worked through. Immediate family and friends would notice their lives changing as well, as they struggled to see a man who was so active before, needing their support every day.

Jeff's life has had its tough moments, especially after the accident. Actually, at times it has been brutal. Jeff's self-perception was totally destroyed, as he struggled to identify with the person he now was. He has been depressed at times as he considered the uncertainty of his situation. Jeff's diminished sense of self was sometimes confirmed by the reactions of people around him. They were responding to a person who had completely changed—a common characteristic of people with severe brain injuries. Jeff's brain injury would have a lifelong impact. He has endured fifteen years of intense, seemingly never-ending rehabilitation, and excruciating pain in his left arm, which was paralyzed. Jeff struggled to regain use of this arm but eventually decided to have it amputated. While the sensation of his phantom limb was at times disturbing and painful, Jeff has approached this experience, living life with one arm, head on.

Whether it be spending an afternoon rock climbing, driving his car for an afternoon trip to the beach or typing 30 words per minute with one hand Jeff is determined to live life to the fullest. Since this accident, Jeff's life has taken a new direction. He has learned many insights, which he is going to share with you. They have come through prayer, spirituality, seminars by Dr. Wayne Dyer, the Landmark Education Program, and inspirational poetry.

Life Is An Opportunity

✦

These varied connections have helped Jeff accept himself as he faces the challenges of each day. These connections have been sources of empowerment to Jeff. Through them, he has been able to achieve inner peace even while living with the effects of a severe brain injury and an amputated left arm. Jeff's spiritual connection was strengthened when talking to the Pastor at a new church he found in Kitchener. Pastor Ken and all of the people at this church were a strong continual support to Jeff and were a crucial element to Jeff developing this self-acceptance. This has been an ongoing support for him over the past 15 years. As a result of Jeff's self-acceptance, many opportunities have come into his life. He hopes the same will happen to you.

Finding It Out There

I twiddle my thumbs and pull my hair,
I can't see any opportunity out there.
People say to look harder and I will see,
But I'm staring and all I can see is me!

Does this sound like something you do too?
So immersed in your life that
it doesn't really seem to matter how you try.
People just say 'hi' and then 'bye- bye.'
They just want to know the surface me.

But taking off the blinders and looking beyond me,
I can see the opportunity that's there to see.
Places I can use the experiences
I've gone through or even what I do,
And even offer a hand, maybe to help you too.

Taking my eyes off myself I can see all of the possibility!

Jeff Martin

For Jeff, it was tough moving forward after the accident, very tough. Because of a tiny dip in the road, a young man had a freak accident that changed his life and lost everything he had achieved to date.

Through countless hours of meditation and prayer, Jeff has come to understand the possibility of who he could be and what he wanted to be respected for. Jeff's view of himself had shifted. This shift allowed Jeff to take the focus off himself and see the opportunities that were there for him. Jeff hopes that you will be able to do this for yourself as well.

Jeff has received great advice from those who love and care for him. At one point, Jeff couldn't even think straight or sort things out for himself. He greatly appreciated the help offered by others during these trying periods. The guidance given by loved ones was crucial for a man who was starting life again from the ground up.

Jeff is now able to decide for himself what he wants for his life. He has improved far beyond what anyone thought possible. Despite his initial bleak medical prognosis, Jeff now lives in his own house in Kitchener. He remains in therapy, though not as intense as before. He has completed a College Certificate in Educational Assistance and is currently pursuing other opportunities at Conestoga College. With the support and encouragement of friends and family, Jeff has continued to find opportunity in his life. How else could you search opportunities in your life to reach the goals you want to achieve? Do you have these goals set before you? Is this something you could work toward? Working this way helps to keep you focused moving forward seeing opportunity each day.

While Jeff has done extremely well since the accident and leads an independent life, for a long time he felt as though something was missing. This realization came to him after he read a quote by Martin Luther King Jr.: "An individual has not started living until he can rise above the narrow confines of his individualistic concerns to the broader concerns of all humanity."[1] This was so intensely commanding, that Jeff began studying the man who marked history in such a powerful way. The quote states that life doesn't begin until you reach beyond yourself to the world around you. This awareness was the final impetus for this book.

The following is a collection of poems written by me, poems by other authors as noted, my reflections on these poems, and related insights which have come to me. Please take into your life whatever is revealed to you. I hope when you open the doors to look at yourself, you are able to see the beautiful person that you are and were meant to be.

Getting Your Perspective Right

✦

The journey to find the person you were meant to be can be examined in the context of the poem, *Footprints*.[2] The footprints in the sand mark the journey we have taken in our life. These prints are markers of how connected we are to our spiritual selves and represent the moments when life simply flows, when one set of footprints marks the way. This is when we are working with Him.

Footprints

One night I dreamed
I was walking along the beach with the Lord.
Many scenes from my life flashed across the sky.
In each scene I noticed footprints in the sand.
Sometimes there were two sets of footprints,
other times there were one set of footprints.

This bothered me because I noticed
that during the low periods of my life,
when I was suffering from
anguish, sorrow or defeat,
I could see only one set of footprints.

So I said to the Lord,
"You promised me Lord,
that if I followed you,
you would walk with me always.
But I have noticed that during
the most trying periods of my life
there have only been one
set of footprints in the sand.
Why, when I needed you most,
you have not been there for me?"

The Lord replied,
"The times when you have
seen only one set of footprints in the sand,
is when I carried you."

—Mary Stevenson

Serenity Prayer

God grant me the serenity
to accept the things I cannot change;
courage to change the things I can;
and wisdom to know the difference.

—Reinhold Niebuhr[3]

A shift to see that it is the journey which counts, and how we get to wherever it is we are going, is where your focus needs to stay. Life is about the journey, not about the destination. Often this true focus is not held, but reversed with concern of where we will get to next. Do you find that too, always wishing you were somewhere else with your focus on where you'll get to next? With the correct view, trusting that through connection to your spiritual selves you are always exactly where you are supposed to be, the journey of your lifetime will be in focus. This is felt through the confidence and freedom when life flows, when you can't help but trust your instincts, and you look back and see one set of footprints marking the way!

Here's another analogy: life is like an orchestra while people are like violin strings. Find those who work and play in harmony with you. These people will build you up and you will build them up too. You will notice that flow starting to appear, when the sounds just blend. Respect their opinions but be true to the sound your violin string was meant to be. When played together all of these true sounds will form a symphony, the symphony that life was meant to be.

Keep your focus on the journey of life, with your spiritual connection in tact. Surround yourself with others who are focused as well. You will build them up and they will build you up too. Find the place where you see one set of footprints marking the way in the sand, a place where you feel His arms around you and a place where life has an endless flow to it.

Walking along the path of life, how often do you look back and see one set of footprints? Are you trying to make the journey all by yourself (as many people do) or when you look back, do you feel His arms around you? When you look at the footprints in the sand, what do you see? Do they mark a journey uncovering the beauty of who you are, or are there two sets of footprints in the sand? I hope this book will give you some insight into your own life. After reading it, I hope you too look back, for at least part of your journey, and observe the moments when life simply flows and there is but one set of footprints marking the way.

Change your perspective and tune in to the intuitive abilities you naturally have. Find these abilities and let life flow beyond your personal boundaries. This is what life is about.

It is so easy to despair about the unfortunate circumstances we sometimes find ourselves in, or to dwell on misery yet to come. Do you find that too, moving into this pitfall all too often? Do you even find yourself dwelling on the projected misery yet to come? For me, overcoming this attitude of despair has been an overwhelming accomplishment. I know for many other people it would be as well. Instead of projecting misery into your life, try looking at your situation for what it is and build on the opportunity that lies there. Understand a situation for what it is, accept the reality of things we can't change and know where to use your energies. Realizing this can be immensely freeing. You will stop wasting time and energy on issues you can't change.

Take a situation that you are emotional about, and consider what has gone on or is going on in that situation. Now separate your emotions from that situation. Seriously, take out the fact that you are upset, angry, or a whole list of other emotions that could be the case. That's not to say you shouldn't be, but just think about what actually happened in that situation. Think about it. So what really happened? Seeing this clarity in situations isn't easy when emotions are strong, but when you work on it and practice it, it's freeing. Let your mind instinctively focus on the reality of situations, emotions aside, even though they are tough. **Awesome**.

Keep your focus on the reality of things. Find the place where you see one set of footprints marking the way in the sand, a place where life seems to have an endless flow to it.

Tomorrow's Crest

✦

Finding clarity of vision to see things the way they actually are will allow you to save energy that might have been otherwise wasted by dwelling on the emotional aspects of a situation. Once you change your focus you can begin to enjoy the journey of life and everything that is there for you. With this acuity you will be given the opportunity to see possibilities in situations that once left you entangled with emotion. Keep this thought in mind when you read the next poem.

A Seagull's Flight

August 02, 2002

The rising sun
With potential, even though it is unseen,
Slowly peeking through.

Whispering above the edge.
A new day is about to dawn.
A soft glimmer begins to shine through.

The crashing waves do not disturb.
Tranquility poised on the horizon's crest.
The seagull flies but unable still.

The altitude developing,
We are able to see,
The whisper's edge revealing possibility.

A brilliant presentation
Of potential we first couldn't see.
Now in full bloom, the commotion is hid so deep.

Colors blending,
An orchestra it looks to me.
The potential achieved and surpassed.

The seagulls continue to argue and bicker,
'Til the late ends they do depart.
The radiance dimmed to dusk.

Looking out, off the windowsill,
You can pray knowing that,
Even though you cannot see,

Tomorrow's crest holds the whisper of possibility.

—Jeff Martin

This poem rings true for the direction and attitude Jeff took toward life. How does it resonate for you? Do you search for possibility each day? This poem is about new beginnings, filled with possibility and opportunity!

Can you see any truth to this next statement? In life, most of us are focused on meeting the right person instead of becoming the right person—that is, the person we naturally are. Often we get so caught up in making a good impression on other people that we lose who we are and what we want to stand for.

On any given day, do you behave how people expect you to, or are you a reflection of the person you found when you saw your true character, ability, and connection with God? Are you seeing the possibility in the person you are, each day? Our perception of self begins to form as we are brought into this world, with that first posterior smack in the delivery room. This shocking sensation is followed by the feeling of comfort, as people meet our every need.

What a perspective to start from! Even now, as you read this book, do you notice in your world today how life seems to contradict? Work hard and you'll enjoy retirement early. With the economic downturn, however, some people's retirement savings have dwindled to nothing. Or how about this—your parents tell you if you continue being the "right" person, your life's partner will come to you. Being the right person is only part of the puzzle, but is often projected as the totality of the situation. Life is full of paradoxes, and we have to discover our true character, ability, and connection with God and remain focused seeing this as our possibility.

Clearing away what distracts you from understanding your true character and purpose in life, as the next poem makes clear, can be a confusing process. Make sure you find the person you want to stand for. Be enthusiastic about life, and keep this foundation of who you are. Of course, there will be little bleeps along the way but hold to your foundation. Looking at your strengths and connection to God, change your perspectives and tune it into the intuitive abilities you naturally have. Find them, let life flow beyond your personal boundaries. This is what life is about. Reach out, make this connection and hold it in your sight.

If you make mistakes (as everyone does) move forward and learn from them (which many do not). Not being able to see things for the way they are and reliving the emotions you felt in situations in the past will distort your sense of who you are as an individual. This distortion comes as you often draw personal meaning from the mistakes that were made. With the focus on the past you let the opportunities, that are here now, pass you by.

People make mistakes; it happens. If you constantly dwell on your mistakes, however, you end up trying to walk while looking backwards, as others run forward past you. Keep the forward view in life searching for the crest of tomorrow's possibility.

Missing The Good Stuff

✦

Keep the focus where it should be, on the present, and this awareness will give you the opportunity to see the ability you have right now. With this focus gone, looking at our past, we are unable to see the positive qualities and abilities we have right now. Often, we are so focused on the difficult times we have endured, the scars of our souls, that we miss all the good things about ourselves and about others too.

Confusion

The sea of life is all about,
Encircling all,
Leaving none out.

At times the roughness found within
Disturbs us so,
We don't know where to go.

Lost all about,
We circle around,
So lost we can't be found.

While the loneliness stares at us
Scared so thin,
We wander all about.

Lost in the sea of life
Unable to see
I missed the point …

It's gone from me.

—Jeff Martin

The Patience Prayer

God grant me patience …
And I want it right now!

—Richard Vegas[4]

Living life while working through difficult times happens to everyone. Life has its struggles, but it also has good times too. It's a matter of being able to shift your focus off the tough times and remind yourself of the good ones you've had as well. Can you create this awareness for yourself? An awareness that you are provided for. Looking at those good times and seeing your character that shines through. Also, looking at the tough ones and finding what got you through. I hope that in many respects the insights shared in this book will give you access to see those moments of strength and ability, which are there for you to see.

Going through fifteen years of rehabilitation to get to the point where I could live independently, with out the constant care of other people was very trying. Finding and keeping this focus, on my abilities, is something that I have had to do. Where is your focus in life? Are you looking for your abilities every day? Family and friends alike have been a great support, as has the spiritual connection I have found. What sources do you have that can be of support to you? You've come this far, something has helped you through. Look for your abilities and how you can use them further in your life today. You have these abilities, notice how you have used them in your life in the past and discover how you could harness them more in your life today. As well, observe how you use them in your life: at the homeless shelter or being a motivation to those in the work place. See how they can be used further to make the world around you a better place today.

Does Life Seem like a Routine?

✦

The commotion in life, or the routine of life, however you want to put it, tends to occupy the majority of our time. Isn't that true for you, too? How do you spend your day? I find that often with our time spent on the routine of things, we lose a sense of purpose in our being; the purpose we are born with gets lost. Where did it go? Did it disappear or do I simply have to reconnect with it? Do you ever notice how routine can cause every day to blend together? You know the routine of each day, but it does not inspire you.

I'm not a has-been, I'm a will be.

—Lauren Bacall[5]

A right delayed is a right denied.

—Martin Luther King Jr.[6]

The Walk of Silence

December 23, 2000

Let it go and come with Me!
Our pain surrounds,
Encompassing every aspect of our life.

Really it's okay, forget it ever happened.
We tend to dwell on the past,
Reminding ourselves of troubles gone through.

Find the trust and you will see.
Let go of the hurts gone through
Really, it's hard to do.

Find it in your heart to forgive

13

The wrong done unto you.
One step closer you have come.

Learn to forgive the wrong done unto you.
Forget it and leave it behind.
Closer you will be to going on this walk with Me.

Closer still you must come.
Allow yourself to let it go.
Away from that pain which surrounds.

When this pain is finally freed.
Finally … let go.
You will see

You can now go on this walk with Me.

—Jeff Martin

Do the things you do each day grab hold of you, or are you trying to grab hold of them? Are you trying to create your purpose so it fits what you want it to be, or are you in the process of realizing what it naturally is? When was the last time you sat down and really thought about your purpose in life, or better yet, what difference you could make in the world that day, that week, or that month? Try to begin the day with a thank-you for the opportunity that is there. Ask yourself, "What difference can I make in my community today?" As the last poem indicates once you are in this frame of mind you will be ready to go on a walk with Him. Walking hand in hand with Him, you will be focused on the journey in your life.

Your life is not a routine; don't let it pass you by. Let the journey capture you and see where you are led with all the potential you have. You have it, I have it, we all do! Extend yourself beyond you, be that difference you want to see in the world around you, that's your right. Capture it, be captured by it and don't let the opportunity pass you by.

Recognize those moments when you feel inspired, get happy shivers, or feel goose bumps down your spine. Built into these moments, I propose, are your true abilities. These are the moments when you are expressing or experiencing the awesomeness of what you can be and were meant to be. Capture these moments, because there are many of them. Recognize what is a catalyst to those goose bumps or those shivers, and build that into your day, every day. In this way you will be building inspiration and spiritual connection into every day and having that effect on those around you too.

Simply being with the spiritual connection of where you come from must have an effect on those around you. For example, do you find it difficult to be happy when people around you are grumpy or angry or upset? Well, the opposite is true as well. Stay focused on where you come from and what you want to stand for. When you have those goose bump moments, you will stand out in a good way because others notice it too. For example, when I have been in this space of connectedness I've had people walk right up to me as I'm dancing in a club and ask me questions. They want to know how I maintain my spunky personality, despite my physical challenges. The expression of my connection to the person I want to stand for caught people's attention. I explain, yes, I have one arm, but that is not where my attention is. I'm at the club to have fun and dance, and that's what I'm going to do. I'm not going to let my emotions about my situation take that opportunity away from me. How are your emotions blocking opportunities in your life today? Seriously think about it. What can you do to uncover or see these opportunities? Don't get tangled up in the emotions about the situation; instead, be the person you've found, and see where you are led.

With the ability to see things for how they actually are, you can focus on opportunities in the journey of your life and identify the person you want to be and be respected for. For myself, this means not letting my emotions take away the opportunity to dance and have fun, despite having only one arm. Do you let your emotions block opportunities in your life? Seriously think about it. Recognizing this and taking action will enable you to leave the past behind, enjoy the present and realize a better future.

Everyone is born with an inherent purpose. Finding your life's purpose is a journey many embark on, but few see to the end. I found my own purpose when I realized it was time for something bigger, much bigger, to start happening in my life. At this point, I had spent about 15 years in rehabilitation from the accident I was involved in.

I made a large step toward discovering my purpose when I attended the Landmark Education Program in Toronto.[7] This Program helped me uncover the role I had so diligently held onto and played for almost 34 years. This process involved a discovery of my true self, by clearing away all the things that masked my abilities and personality. Since Landmark, my life has changed dramatically. I can see the opportunities in life, which before were not apparent to me. If you are reading this book and have never heard of the Landmark Education Program, it might be worth checking out.

Keeping the forward view in life is important, because that's what we want to move towards, and is often thwarted when people look back and dwell on past events. Seeing life, as an opportunity is the perspective life should evolve from. With this as the background, problems can be dealt with reflected on and the past can be left exactly there, in the past.

Being The Difference You Want to See

✦

A shift in perspective in how you look at things will help you see the possibilities in every day. With a shift to see the world through the window of love, understanding this is where you came from, you will capture the possibilities that are there for you every day. Making this shift realizes a promise made, as conveyed in the following poem.

A Promise

A time of commencement
And a time of completion.
With endless possibilities found between.
These experiences found, what are they to be?

These possibilities existing
Are often overshadowed by the uncertainty of what will be.
Perhaps seeming to want to drag us down.
Why does it seem to depress us so?

This uncertainty as to what life will be.
But why does it always seem to happen to me?
Damn it, I'm sick and tired of the burdens I always seem to bear.
It's a consciousness that always seems to be there.

Try not to count the curses (or at least they seem) you're subject to.
But concentrate on the blessings God has given you.
Just shift your focus so you can see.

It's not what you do that matters the most,
The difference is our perception of these times conquered through.
In every situation you face each day,
look for the promise that has been given.
God's sworn blessing is hiding within.

Tell someone you love them; be compassionate, not cruel,
as life may seem to be.
Help them shift their focus
From something they don't want to bear.
Let them know you really do care.

Give someone help … let them know what they mean to you.
All they want is an edge, something to help them through.
Really, what do they mean to you?
This confidence gives them an edge, don't you see?

If I can let you know what you mean to me,
Perhaps then your eyes will be opened to see.
Knowing that you are accepted for the child you were meant to be.
Get out of the racing mode and just be.

Life is not made of the experiences found within
But your perception of which, this matters most.
Being productive without losing who you are and falling into a spin
Get out of the racing mode and don't just coast.

This freedom is what will let you be,
all this I've said here now and today
You've helped me see.
Life … is not what life appears to be.
Let me be happy to just be me.

—Jeff Martin

Ever notice how easy it is to dwell on negative events in the past? Not to simply reflect but dwell. That is really a tough issue for me. It is our right to learn from past mistakes and move forward, leaving the experience behind us. But too often don't you find yourself imagining what could have happened in a situation or even what could happen in a situation that hasn't occurred yet? You don't know what is going to happen, but you almost instinctively project the worst-case scenario into your life.

No wonder life seems so difficult. We are trying to predict the outcomes for life and living into the prediction of something that isn't, but could be! No wonder we're stressed all the time. Does this sound familiar to you? All that time wasted on something that hasn't taken place yet. Sounds pretty dumb to me. Don't get me wrong; I used to do it to and still do it now.

Why not look at the situation for what it is, seeing and building on the opportunity that lies there? Why stress yourself out about something that might be? Try instead to let life flow. As Niebuhr wrote in the Serenity Prayer, "God grant me the serenity to accept the things I cannot change, courage to change the things I can, and wisdom to know the difference." Through this knowledge and wisdom, put your energies into something that will make a difference, so you can be the difference. As Gandhi said, "Be the difference you want to see in the world." Or, as Lauren Bacall put it, "I'm not a has-been, I'm a will-be." It's your life, isn't it?

Life is wonderful. Life is great, but anyone who is in touch with reality knows that life has its challenges and can be very difficult at times. But why is that? If we are in touch with our spiritual source, why are we so stressed? Do you notice that there seems to be no flow to your life? The moments of inspiration have dwindled, if not disappeared. Have you ever felt this flow before; those times where things just feel right and seem to fall into place?

To find this spot where things seem to just flow, I think about this affirmation every morning: *"I open my heart and sing the joys of love."* A true friend, one of the angels in my life, helped me develop this affirmation. With this affirmation each morning, I begin with the proper foundation to allow life to flow from it. If you started each day and held that affirmation or idea in your mind, how would your thought process change? Think about it for a second. If you approached people that you don't get along with very well with the attitude, *"I open my heart and sing the joys of love,"* how would they respond? How would you respond? Try this as an approach to every day.

Remember that the destination isn't the focus, the journey we travel on and how we get there, is. Letting go of the past is difficult as you often live with the results today. Dealing with the past, and shifting your focus to where you are going with your current situation, allows you to focus on opportunities that are there for you now. By remaining present, rather than dwelling on past stressors and being emotionally tangled up in them, you will be able to deal with the effects of past decisions. You will be able to look and move forward.

Who's the Expert Now?

✦

Emotions are so complex and tough to work through. Another aspect is how people attach emotions to the outcome of an event and play on that emotion? They almost make the emotion the essence of what is happening, at least in their minds. For example, when watching the Stanley Cup, you're cheering for your team and excitement grows with the anticipation, and your team scores a goal! Popcorn, beer, and chips fly everywhere, it's a colossal celebration. When someone scores against your team: *Agghh*! You're in agony. You can't possibly see how he could have scored that goal. Apparently, you are now the expert in hockey and know exactly what your team should have done to prevent that goal. Oh yes, and you also know exactly how they should have scored too!

These emotions become your reality. Can you picture situations in your life where the emotions are the reality of what you are experiencing? How does this change or cloud your perception of what is actually happening? Creating this clarity will help you to discover the place of serenity that is there in each of us. When you are living your emotions seeing the realities of situations, and your ability to reach other people does not become a common sense response. Let this open to you as you reflect on the following two poems.

> An individual has not started living until he can rise above the narrow confines of his individualistic concerns to the broader concerns of all humanity.
>
> —Martin Luther King Jr.

Humpty With Attitude

Humpty Dumpty sat on a wall
What was he doing there anyway?
He knows better 'cause—
Whoops, off he goes.

Splat! All over the ground
Now once again what were you thinking, Humpty?
Here comes all the king's horses and all the king's men
To put Humpty back together again!

Several days later, all the King's men asked Humpty again,
What were you doing on that wall, you silly old fool?
Before you try anything like that again think about the fact
we're not going to put Humpty back together again.

—Jeff Martin

Be conscious of and don't overplay life situations. Use common sense in the things that you do; think them through. Do you find yourself at work spreading gossip about other coworkers or complaining about job-related stress, or how other drivers on the way home were going so slow you had to speed, which is why you got a speeding ticket … etc, etc. In reality, what happened was a coworker made a mistake, your day didn't flow effortlessly and you got a speeding ticket. How does your perception of what has really happened in these situations affect the reality of what you are experiencing? Are you stressing yourself out?

What about this scenario: you get laid off at work. "Oh shoot" is the response (perhaps more dramatic but is the direction of the comments nonetheless) "I'm out of a job!" Yeah, it sucks; change sucks—or at least while the change is taking place it does. What does this mean? No one expects you to be deliriously happy in this situation, but challenge yourself to look for the opportunity in a situation. How the heck can you see the possibility in that? Sounds like mumbo-jumbo, good-feeling stuff, right? In a lot of respects it does sound like exactly that, I totally agree with you.

While looking for new work may be a pain in the posterior, it may lead into a better paying job or the possibility for further promotions. You don't know. Don't ignore the reality of the situation, but take it as an opportunity and try it like that. Working so that it is a common sense response, seeing situations as opportunities, **awesome!** People, friends, and family may bond closer together to help you out, and who knows what might develop in those relationships. What you have is an open book of opportunity, and it is up to you to decide what you will do with it. You don't know what will happen, but there is no sense in playing out the worst-case scenario.

By imagining the worst-case scenario, you might actually be laying the foundation of failure (the exact thing you don't want). This is often referred to as a self-fulfilling prophecy. When you notice those around you in these situations, support them and they will instinctively be there to support you also. That is what you would want for you, so do it for someone else too.

The culminating incident in my life, as mentioned in the section of this book The Last Straw, was a very serious motorcycle accident. This situation, as terrible and catastrophic as it was, brought everyone in my family closer together. My recovery was very difficult and I required support from family and friends alike. They had to be and were a support for each other too. As I struggled through the initial stages of a serious brain injury, coupled with the paralysis of my left arm (and eventual amputation) this support was encouraging and essential for me.

This change required a relearning and redefining of life. It gave me the opportunity to find and use my strengths. Seeing my situation as an opportunity is something I've learned to do. It was necessary. Change will be difficult at first, but you will need to search for new skills and find your strengths. Look for these abilities. Find them and open up to them, use them, and help others by using them too. By reaching out to others in this way you are actually reaching in and opening the possibilities of your natural abilities, using them and strengthening them, now that is **awesome**.

I have been able to help someone in my life's path. The person I assisted had unhealthy behavior and thinking patterns, which were masking or hiding his ability and spiritual connection. My help resulted in him changing in a positive way. This has come back to me, not in the same way I helped him out, but in ways far greater than I could have ever expected.

Being a support to others and exercising our strengths allows our true selves to come out. When we reach out to others without expecting anything in return, we find our strengths. Working from your inner self, your abilities will be manifested in the world around you. Your shift in perspective will take place, as you become that difference you've wanted to see. With this connection intact, you will be coming from that place of *NEW BEGINNINGS*; this is the life you've been searching for.

Using your abilities and helping other people is the starting point to actually living life. By taking your focus off yourself, you can realize your own potential and be the difference you've wanted to see.

Recognizing your strengths and your purpose in life is inspiring, but putting them into action, so others benefit, is where real empowerment begins. Use your abilities wisely and you will not go unnoticed. Working toward letting these abilities flow is when you start the real journey of living, with one set of footprints marking the way.

Are You a Collage of Opinions?

◆

Do the expectations others have of you cloud the footprints you make in the sand? Have you noticed we often take others' expectations on and direct our lives by what we are expected to do or better yet, by what other's think would make us happier? Think about the last time you bought a dress or a suit. Did you find yourself asking other people, even people you didn't know, how does it look? Actually how do you think it looks? Quit ignoring your own opinion; it's yours and it matters. We often take it upon ourselves to make changes based on the opinions of others, with little reflection on our own. The expectations others have of us too often determines the person we think we are.

Windows To Our Soul

A deadly stare, long and hard.
They reach into your heart,
Searching for some companionship.
So mysterious yet longing to be understood.

They understand and interpret so much,
Yet are still lost.
Lost in the world surrounding and hiding
The true compassion found within.

These mysterious tunnels are something we all own,
and are a true reflection of what can be found within.
Of course, this true reflection of personality
is found in one's eyes.

Jeff Martin

How we see the world is changed by the person we are; it alters our perspective. If you put too much weight on the opinions of others and don't take time to reflect on your own, are you simply a collage of other people's opinions? Holy smokes! Does this describe you? It's important to be aware of other people's opinions, but also be conscious of and give importance to your own as well.

Our life experiences shape our personality. A scolding finger from a parental figure, constantly repeated, tells us we are not accepted or that we are always wrong. Being endlessly surrounded by love tells us we are loved and worthy of love. Witnessing violence in the home or community tells us violence is acceptable. Experiencing encouragement provides a catalyst for us to be fearless in the life we are creating for ourselves. From these experiences we perceive the world accordingly. Our eyes are often referred to as windows to our souls. As mentioned in the poem, our eyes allow us to see things in the world, but how we perceive the world is determined by the person we are.

This next phrase summarizes the point well: "Finally being able to see that you are becoming the person you are, not the person you thought you should be, you are free." Finding this recognition amid all the expectations and distractions of every day gives you freedom to just be.

The journey of discovering this person is described in the next two poems. Identifying yourself amid the collage of life and standing for the person you find when looking at your true character, your abilities and your connection to God is where life should evolve from. Living life from this perspective is a way to make sure you can get and give the most in your life today. Remain focused and make sure the opportunity doesn't slip by. You are given lots of advice in life from those who love and care for you. Take these ideas and reflect on them but make sure you don't lose the essence of who you are. If you have trouble with this, when people impose their opinions on you, understand their intention. Find the love that is there in the suggestions, but reflect on your own, too. Use that as your basis as you accept the love that has been given. Be aware that you don't want to become a collage of other people's opinions. It's your life; find the person you want to stand for, acknowledge that person, and return the love to that person who has given the gift of love to you.

The eyes are often referred to as windows of the soul. You see the world with your eyes, but what you perceive is dependent on who you are. See the love that is there all around you. Look for it and find it. Keep this as your window to the world.

As the poem in this section notes, the essence of your ability is found in your connection to God. He comes from love and so do you. Once you find that true connection within, you will be closer to finding that connection with Him.

Be conscious of the perceptions you have from life experiences. Connect to that inner self and use love as your light. With love being the foundation you come from every day, like in the affirmation I start every day with, you will be emanating a selfless perspective. Living with this approach, as noted by Dr. King, is the marking of when life truly begins. Extend yourself beyond you, to people around: open the door for them, and if they are shortchanged at the store, it's not going to break you to spot them a few pennies. Be conscious of only saying good things behind someone's back.

Create these habits for yourself, and others will follow. If you saw other people doing this, how would it affect you? Given that this presence of love is addictive, imagine what could happen. Go forward from the standpoint of love in your life, and imagine what you can attract!

Are You Still Searching?

✦

Do you find that you search for different ways to be happy? I think everyone does. But in that search, where do you look? To a car, house, girlfriend or boyfriend or a spouse? Happiness does not come through acquiring something, or even someone, but by realizing and appreciating who you are. Isn't that the case for you too? Excitement grows as you are about to buy a new car, you get the car and a month later you are back to the same old routine. How else does this play in your life? Find an appreciation for the important things in your life and keep this as your focus.

Confusion

[You read this poem already,
but I had to add it here with a few extras.]

The sea of life is all about,
Encircling all,
leaving none out.

At times the roughness found within,
Disturbs us so,
We don't know where to go.

Lost all about,
We circle around,
So lost we can't be found.

Once we uncover the routines we can see the person we
naturally are.

While the loneliness stares at us
Scared so thin,
We wander all about.

Sound familiar, searching everywhere for happiness. You have it one minute but then it's gone the next, so you look some more, over and over again. Of course that scares you, it scares me too!

Lost in the sea of life
Unable to see
I missed the point…
It's gone from me.

Capture the important things in life and recognize all of the
opportunity there is, before it's gone from you.

—Jeff Martin

Destiny Revealed

Life's soaring seas wandering all about,
There is no direction to guide the spiritual self.
You are lost, wondering where it is you have to go.
Looking desperately for a place to hide.

Searching for a blanket to give you comfort,
Not knowing if it is to be found,
You search all around.
Rising up, the problems surround.

Encircled by all,
Not knowing where to go,
You curl up with prayers.
Continuing with no purpose in mind.

You are guided around, up and down.
Perhaps still not knowing why, you carry on.
The persistence assured it seems.
Immovable in purpose, driven by passion.

Change brought about by the faith within.
The obsession, its purpose becoming clear.
There is nothing to find out here.

You may ask,
So why are we searching?
And I will tell you
The answer is found within.

—Jeff Martin

Again, it is not the destination we should be focused on, but rather the journey you go through to get there. A focus on God as your source of every day helps to keep the journey in view, with the proper perspective of you. If you keep this perspective in sight, you will search within for this connection, as Martin Luther King Jr. says, to be a co-worker with God.

It is easy to be distracted or over-immersed in life and material things. More often than not, people search all around them to find happiness or their purpose in life. Find that internal compass or connection to your spiritual self, and use it as a marker for new beginnings.

> Somewhere we must come to see that human progress never
> rolls in on the wheels of inevitability. It comes through the
> tireless effort and the persistent work of dedicated individuals
> who are willing to be coworkers with God.
>
> —Martin Luther King Jr.[8]

Connecting to your spiritual inner self will get you to that point where life simply flows. Starting each day from the perspective, 'as a coworker with God', you will allow life to flow from it. Life can be awesome; life can be great. It's in your perspective that the shift takes place. Often your life is filled with questions about why we go through our routines each day, and what purpose we have in life. Everyone of us has a purpose. Each of us has strengths, but as the world seems so competitive, we often focus on comparing the negatives.

Why look for the negative? Why not find the positive in everyone else, and build them up? Get your mind off yourself and build others. By doing so, you're reaching out and making a difference in their lives. As you do this selflessly, it gets your mind off yourself. When others build you up, take it in and give the credit that is due. When passed along it will only magnify. This true connection, extending beyond yourself, will leave you at peace with a realized, positive, self-fulfilling prophecy.

Success is not measured by the money or number of material things we are able to accumulate, but by the level to which a person is able to discover their purpose and use it in their lives and the lives of others. This discovery is what this book is all about and will only magnify as it is passed along. Working together, not against one another, is something that should come naturally. Imagine the difference that would make in your life or the lives of others. Imagine where that could lead!

Getting Your Importance Straight

✦

As the next poem indicates, a speck in the world is often how we feel but is not what you were meant to be. Everyone has a purpose and innate abilities to make a difference in the world. This difference will be magnified as we work together to try to build each other up. If we build others up, they will instinctively build us up too.

A Little Speck

A little speck encircled by all.
It feels so tiny no one seems to notice at all.
Seeming to be lost in the chaos of life's sea.

But there is love all around the little speck to see,
Something hard for the speck to do.
Perhaps unconscious of it but still surrounded to see.

This confusion in life distracting the speck so,
In all honesty, it doesn't know where to go!
It's lonely and tired, life seems to go amiss.

Life for this little speck is uncertainty, definitely to be.
How does what appears to be a little speck live it fully through?
Does this little speck make a difference to you?

Again reminded about the uncertainty, what to do?
Hard to feel certainty without feeling a little Mr. Magoo.
Questions. Questions. Questions.

It has no answers, which are easily found.
Just questions begging for it to see.
How does a little speck live life as it was meant to be?

The speck goes here, the speck goes there.
Its seems to have gone everywhere.
All around it tries to be but is still unable to see.

I often feel like a little speck and am sure you do too.
Discovering the importance of you and of me
is something we have to see.
Get this to be something that comes naturally.

Many specks in the world make this a better place to be.
If you can only make a difference in a little speck's life today,
you will finally be able to see.

A speck in the world is not all you were meant to be!

—Jeff Martin

When we come into this world, we see nothing but possibility. The world seems centered around us. People poke and prod you and smiles and giggles are the energy that surrounds. People saw your possibility. **Continue to see that possibility in life**. We are lovable and have potential, regardless of who we are. Remember that what happens in the world is seen differently by each person. Our life experiences and the people we have become alter our perspectives. Change the view of yourself. Your potential is there; it's in you, and it's waiting for you to discover and see. You were, and are still, a great bundle of joy. Find your joy in life, the love in your life, and find the purpose that pulls at you.

Connecting to your inner self and your abilities gives your life purpose.

Let the reflections shared here become part of the person you are. Let your abilities and your connection to God be the source of change and *NEW BEGINNINGS* within yourself. By shifting your focus and living life from this perspective, you can see what you want to stand for and want to be respected for. Be the difference you want to see. Hold yourself accountable. Continue to see your possibility. This is the way life should be, a life of being the difference you want to see.

Find where life flows and see where the next step takes you!

You can read all you want, but if you don't put it into practice in your life, then of course nothing will happen. As you read the reflections, let them merge with the person you are, and put them into practice. As the last verse says, see where the next step takes you.

Acknowledgments

Editing on the pictures and technical data done by **Justin Ballantyne**.

General editing in the beginning stages by **Marietta Buell**.

Final editing for the book completed by **Nate Hendley**

I do want to acknowledge the dedication of my friend **Ruth Peter**. Her knowledge, guidance and help with this book could not be replaced.

Thank you.

References

1. Quotation by Martin Luther King Jr. from www.brainyquote.com/quotes/authors/m/martin_luther_king_jr.html
2. "Footprints" by Mary Stevenson from www.footprints-inthe-sand.com/index.php?page=Poem/Poem.php
3. Serenity Prayer by Reinhold Niebuhr from www.cptryon.org/prayer/special/serenity.html
4. The Patience Prayer by Richard Vegas from http://www.streetdirectory.com/travel_guide/8785/self_improvement_and_motivation/god_grant_me_patienceand_i_want_it_now.html
5. Quotation by Lauren Bacall from www.brainyquote.com/quotes/quotes/l/laurenbaca379179.html
6. Quotation by Martin Luther King Jr. from www.brainyquote.com/quotes/authors/m/martin_luther_king_jr.html
7. Landmark Education International Inc.
    184 Front Street East
    Toronto, ON M5A 4N3, Canada
    (416) 777-2230
8. Quotation by Martin Luther King Jr. from http://smu.edu/newsinfo/stories/mlk-speech-excerpts-1966.asp

**If you have comments you'd like to pass along to me after reading this book, please feel free to do so. **

You can contact me at: <u>empowerment2u@live.com</u>

Thank you